WITH BEST WISHES

CW01661400

JANE AND IDA

BEER LACE MANUFACTURERS TO ROYALTY

S White

HB
Honeybee Books

Honeybee Books

Published by Honeybee Books
Broadoak, Dorset
www.honeybeebooks.co.uk

Printed in the UK using paper from sustainable sources

Front Cover: Courtesy of Glyn Holford

ISBN: 978-1-910616-19-2

Whilst I have endeavoured to obtain copyright permissions and trace and verify all sources of information and acknowledge them, should I have omitted any, I offer my sincere apologies and will happily make amendments upon receipt of further information.

For
Xander Moore
&
Hector Arias Thornton
who never cease to make me smile!

CONTENTS

Illustrations

Appendices

Introduction

I have been an amateur genealogist for several years, interested as much in the social history of people as in the "who begat whom". (Only another genealogist will empathise with the joy of finding a grave!) The very first family that I researched, and am continuing to research, includes the Bidneys and the Allens.

During a visit to a Beer Heritage Exhibition, I wanted to correct some information shown against a photograph of Mrs Allen's Lace Shop. It would have been far easier just to let them have the "family tree", but instead I found myself questioning the "known in the family" information, and the folklore, and became enthralled with the consequential research and findings. This monograph is the result.

It is not about the intricacies of lace and lace making. There are far more knowledgeable authors and experts than I on that subject. Kindly people who have given me their time and honest opinions of this story so far, have described it as a serious piece of research but, with a much wider appeal to those interested in history in general, local history, fashion and textiles. It is a brief snapshot of the lives and times of two ladies, Jane Washbourne, nee Bidney, and Ida Allen, nee Pike. They're related down the years by marriage, both were involved in the lace industry supplying Beer Lace to Royalty and, both are linked to the village of Beer in East Devon.

Like most stories from the past, it is hard to define fact from fiction or folklore. (You can no more believe all that was written in the newspapers of the 1840s than you can in newspapers of today).

Two people recalling the same event will both relate a slightly different story. It's rather like a jigsaw puzzle, without seeing the complete picture on the box lid, all we can do is put pieces together and guess what the missing pieces may look like.

I can't, in this version of "history", mention Beer without mentioning Branscombe. On the brown information road signs, Branscombe is called a "Picturesque Village" and Beer, an "Historic Fishing Village". Although these two villages share a parish boundary, they are separated by deep valleys and narrow roads. Walking along the cliffs from Beer to Branscombe is a two mile walk, with spectacular scenery across Lyme bay. At the time of this "history", villagers would walk or use a donkey/horse and cart along the narrow country lanes and roads. For as long as oral and written history goes back, there are ancient rivalries and grudges between the two villages; rivalries that still continue, but now more in fun than enmity.

I started writing this monograph three years ago and every time I thought I had finished it, a new piece of information came to light. The current information I have about Jane and Ida raises more questions than it answers. More information is still coming in and whilst I am trying to fill in the gaps, this story remains sometimes unsubstantiated and certainly incomplete. Perhaps it will never be finished. If you can add to this story, please let me know.

Soux White
janeandida@gmail.com

Jane Washbourne, nee Bidney

Jane and her Family

Jane was born in Beer, probably sometime in 1802, as she was baptised on 17th September 1802[1]. Her parents were Thomas Bidney (baptised in 1773) and Hannah Newberry[2] (the daughter of Francis and Ann nee Bishop), who married in 1798[3] in Honiton-on-Otter (now Honiton). The Bidney family in Beer can be traced back to the mid 1600s.

Jane's father, Thomas, was the eldest of five children born to Richard Bidney and Hannah Marshall. His siblings were: Elizabeth who married William Farrant, Ann Marshall Bidney who married James Pearce, Richard who died when he was a year old, and Mary who married William Clarke. A Bidney family tree is shown at Appendix 1.

The family were "Dissenters"[4] and when the new congregational chapel in Beer was built in 1855/1856[5] and extended in 1880, they were part of the congregation. A memorial plaque for Jane's cousin Elizabeth Bidney Farrant (1821-1898) can be found on the wall in the Congregational Chapel in Beer. It reads

"In loving memory of Elizabeth Bidney Farrant who was always a friend of this church and worshiped here for 22 years. She was a devoted teacher in the Sabbath School and ever had the welfare of the cause at heart. Steadfast friend, A woman greatly beloved. She entered into rest 30 September 1898 aged 75 years. Erected by her nephew J T Farrant Hawkins."

Jane had an older sister, Mary Ann Bishop Bidney but she died, aged 3, when Jane was only a year old. Her mother also died in the same year, five months after Mary Ann. We don't know why Mary and Hannah[6] died as, at that time, there were no death certificates and the parish burial records did not record the reason for the death.

Jane's father, Thomas, remarried on 17th April 1804[7] to Jane Loyde, nee Knight, a widow. Jane Knight must have been a friend of Thomas' first wife Hannah as Hannah[8] was a witness at her marriage to Richard Loyde[9], a widower, in 1799.

Thomas[10] died just two years later, aged only 33. Again we don't know why he died at such a relatively young age; life expectancy, at that time, was approximately 40 years of age.

Thomas was a shopkeeper, what sort of shop he had or where in Beer or Seaton it was, we don't currently know. Unusually for the time, he made a Will[11]. His estate was valued at "under £800"[12] and his Executors were his widow Jane and Samuel Newbery (sic) who was living at Bovey, not far from Beer. (Although current research doesn't prove that Samuel was a relative of Thomas' first wife, it is quite possible as he was also a witness at their marriage and appears to have lent money to Thomas' second wife.) Thomas' daughter Jane was to receive £200 when she reached the age of 21 and the residue of his Estate after the death, or second marriage, of his widow Jane.

Jane became 21 in 1823 and received what was the equivalent of approximately £22,000 in 2013's money and, in 1843; she inherited the residue of the estate when her step mother died.

We know that Jane was a lace dealer and probably a lace maker herself, following the old bobbin or pillow lace tradition of Beer. We don't know where in Beer she lived but we can guess that it was possibly in Fore Street[13] or Beer Street/ Main Street, (the central road through the village) as it was then called. Her step mother, on the 1841 census, was shown as living on the eastern side of Main Street. According to Edwin[14] (known as Ted) Pike Allen, who was Ida Allen's second child, she lived in Captain Hawkins' House in Main Street. It's a double fronted thatched house dating back to the early 18century. (If you face the sea, the house is on the left hand side just before going down Sea Hill).

Jane and Queen Victoria

Jane seems to have been an educated, entrepreneurial, woman and she probably realised that it would be commercially preferable to sell lace in London rather than in Beer. She already had her own substantial personal income, from her father's estate, and could therefore afford to travel and set up in business.

We don't know when Jane first went to London but we find her at 12 Duke Street, Manchester Square, London in 1834[15] (when she was aged 32 and William IV was King) where she was at "Mr Williams, Linen draper, haberdasher and dealer in lace." Although at Mr Williams' she was most likely already trading in her own right. Perhaps it was the modern day equivalent of a store within a store? She was still in London in 1837[16] but by this time had moved round the corner to 76 St James Street where she is recorded, trading in her own name, as a Dealer in Lace.

Even though Jane had money to support her, can you imagine what it must have been like for a woman, on her own, in the early 1800s to leave a small fishing village and travel to London to set up in business?

Try and imagine the village of Beer: no electricity, no gas lights, no cars, un-metalled roads, carts and horses. The village was dependant on fishing, (Jane's great grandfather Richard, who died before she was born, had a share in a Beer fishing boat called the "Providence"[17]), working the Beer stone quarry, farming, lace making and, of course, smuggling. (The famous Beer Smuggler Jack Rattenbury[18] was still alive). Thatch topped cottages, with small windows, standing shoulder to shoulder, sloping down the street. The dark red sails of the Beer Luggers juxtaposed against the blue green sea. The smell of gutted fish mingled with salty brine and the sound of the tumbling fresh water brook that runs through the village.

Beer Village circa 1885

Looking down Fore Street, towards Sea Hill, some 45 years after the making of Queen Victoria's wedding dress.

Photo courtesy of Seaton Museum

Looking down Fore Street, towards Sea Hill, as it is today.

The Thatched cottages on the right have gone, being replaced with a car park and the "modern end" of the Anchor Inn. Further down the hill on the right, the fisherman's cottages on the hill have also disappeared. Some of the original thatched buildings on the left still exist.

Jane must have travelled to London by stage coach, as the railway stations at Honiton and Axminster did not open until July 1860. The stage coach would probably have started in Exeter and is likely to have followed the coach route on the "new" road from Honiton onto Chard (now the modern A30 up to the A303) which was built by the Honiton and Ilminster Trust. The road is still known by some in the Westcountry as The London Road.

Perhaps from this, the argument arose: was the lace called "Honiton Lace" because the precious lace arrived in London from the marketing centre of Honiton or, because historically, in 1676[19] one third of the lace makers in East Devon lived in Honiton. Personally, I think it was the former, and it is staunchly still called Beer Lace in Beer, but elsewhere others vehemently disagree.

Guildhall, Fore Street, Exeter 1830

Stage coach tracks can be seen on the right with the stage coach in the distance. *From the Devonshire and Cornwall Illustrated courtesy of Alan Rosevear, Turnpikes.org.uk*

Local folk lore suggests that Jane had never been outside Devon before and fainted from nerves whilst waiting to be received by Queen Victoria in London. She probably did faint whilst waiting to be received by the Queen, but as we now know, she was already some years established in business in London.

Pat Earnshaw's[20] "A Dictionary of Lace", states that Jane was appointed "*Honiton Brussels Point Lace Manufacturer*" to Queen Victoria on 14th August 1837. Jane described herself as a "Point Lace Manufacturer"[21], which was actually bobbin lace. The "point" refers to the delicacy of the lace rather than the point of a needle.

We know that Queen Victoria supported the British clothing industry and wanted to support the waning lace industry but why did

Queen Victoria choose Jane as her Lace Manufacturer as there were other lace manufactures around at the same time. We don't know why, but choose her she did.

Records from Queen Victoria's wardrobe accounts show that Jane was paid £12-12-0d during 1837 (approximately £1,200 in 2013's money), and £168-16-0d in 1838 (approximately £16,000 in 2013's money).

Not very long ago I was given three postcards which picture a Mrs Betsey Woodgate, of Beer, of whom it is said that she helped to make Queen Victoria's Coronation dress.

Research revealed that she was Elizabeth Ann Newton[22] baptised on 22 June 1828, the daughter of Henry and Sarah. Betsey would have been just ten years old when she made lace for Queen Victoria's Coronation dress.

The legend on this post card reads "*Hontion Lace Maker Mrs Woodgate of Beer, Aged 82, who helped to make Queen Victoria's Coronation Dress*"

Henry Newton, Betsy Woodgate's father, aged 23, was arrested in 1819 for smuggling in Weymouth and was "*Put on board His Majesty's ship Queen Charlotte in Portsmouth Harbour to be [illegible] in His Majesty's Royal Navy. By the orders of [illegible] Commissioners of His Majesty's Customs.*"[23]).

Betsey married Samuel Henry Woodgate[24], the son of James and Lydia, on 3rd September 1850 and, at the time of her marriage, she was recorded as a "Lacemaker". She was not shown on the 1841 Census[25] as a lace maker, although her mother Sarah was. Betsey must have fallen on hard times, as in 1907, by which time she had been widowed, a letter was written to Buckingham Palace on her behalf. This letter resulted in "*some small pecuniary assistance from His Majesty's Privy Purse has been sent to the Rev Hollis on Mrs Woodgate's behalf.*"[26]

One can only assume that photographs of Betsey were taken and turned into postcards (of which there were several different ones) and sold to also provide her with monetary assistance.

An interesting diversion, but back to Jane. The postcards got me thinking;

a) Jane was resident at 76 St James Street by 1837.
b) Jane had been appointed Lace Manufacturer to the Queen in 1837.
c) Queen Victoria's coronation took place on 28 June 1838.
d) Mrs Woodgate of Beer allegedly made some of the lace for Queen Victoria's coronation robe.

Is it possible that it was Jane who procured Mrs Woodgate's lace for the coronation robe and, was it for this that some of the money in 1837/1838 was paid to Jane? Although, currently, conjecture, perhaps Jane played a part in the making of Queen Victoria's coronation robe as well as in Queen Victoria's wedding dress. Coincidentally, The Globe newspaper of 28th June 1838, reported that the Coronation Procession passed St James Street, so it's likely that Jane was in the crowd watching the coronation procession.

Queen Victoria[27] first met her German cousin, Prince Albert of Saxe-Coburg and Gotha, in 1836, and they became engaged during his second visit to England in October 1839. Queen Victoria recorded in her journal that she had sent for Albert and said to him "*that it would make me too happy if he would consent to what I wanted (that he should marry me). We embraced each other over and over again, and he was so kind and so affectionate.*"[28]

Newspapers from 1840[29] and subsequent research and publications record that it took between 150 and 200 "tailoresses" to make the lace for the dress, working for six or nine months between March and November 1839. The lace for the wedding dress was made up of; the flounce for the dress, which measured 4ft 6" by 2ft 6" attached to the back of the skirt, together with lace frills, a bertha (a long collar worn around the shoulders, leaving the shoulders bare) and a veil which, according some accounts, was a yard and a half square[30].

It therefore seems that Queen Victoria ordered the lace for her wedding dress before she became officially engaged to Prince Albert! However, it is more likely that Queen Victoria ordered the flounce first, to support the lace industry, with the bertha and veil being ordered after her engagement to complete the wedding dress. Queen Victoria's wardrobe accounts show that £34-0-0d was paid to Jane during the second quarter of 1839 (approximately £3,200 in 2013's money) and we presume that this is when the flounce was finished, and that Jane was paid a further £250-0-0d during 1840 (approximately £22,000 in 2013's money).

Newspaper accounts of the time[31] said that at the express wish of Queen Victoria, Jane travelled back to Beer to supervise the making of the lace. Whether or not Queen Victoria told Jane to go back to Beer, is not actually known. It seems just as likely that Jane would wish to return to her home village to supervise such an important commission. Indeed it is highly likely that Jane would have travelled back and forth to Beer regularly in carrying out her business.

William Dyce,[32] a pre-Raphaelite painter, then working at the Government School of Design, at Somerset House, (which became the Royal College of Art) together with an un-named pupil, has now been credited with the design for the lace on Queen Victoria's wedding gown.

In 1983, a letter written by William Dyce to Sir Henry Cole[33] in 1852, making reference to the design of the wedding dress, came to light.

"By the way I have often forgotten to suggest to you to ask the Prince, when you have an opportunity, for a sight of the Queen's marriage dress. It is interesting as the earliest specimen of the old style Brussels point lace executed at Honiton. The design was executed at The School of Design which (i.e. I and one of my pupils) had the merit of effecting the revolution in Honiton lace making which followed the working of the dress."[34]

Following the making of the lace, Jane destroyed the patterns so that the lace could not be copied.

The Flounce of Queen Victoria's Wedding dress
Courtesy of Carol McFadzean and Elizabeth Trebble

Enlarged central section of the flounce of Queen Victoria's wedding dress.
Courtesy of Carol McFadzean and Elizabeth Trebble

Working Conditions

Seeing the lace, ones mind's eye runs riot imagining 100 plus women sitting together with their bobbins clacking working on the lace; rather like an extraordinary quilting session! But where was large enough for 100 women to sit together and, surely no lace pillow was ever large enough! I can hear the guffaws of laughter and disbelief from lace makers at this outrageous suggestion. It was of course, made motif by motif by individuals and these motifs were then delicately sewn together by seamstresses.

The lace makers working conditions were appalling. The delicate lace was made using natural daylight or by candle light. The candles would have been made from tallow (a purified form of beef or mutton fat) as they were cheaper than beeswax. They would have guttered, smoked, smelled and produced a very yellow light. If you were poor, you would have made your own candles by making your own tallow from saved animal fat and using a rush wick. The very poor would have had no light at all. A glass bottle or jar filled with water, placed in front of the candle to enhance and magnify the light was often used when glass could be obtained.

Early photographs and paintings of lace makers show them sitting outside with their pillow and bobbins, using the natural daylight to work by.

This watercolour of **The Lace Maker** by Myles Birket Foster[35] gives a rather sentimental and romantic chocolate-box impression of the work of a lace maker. Reality was far from pretty.

During Lent (the period from Ash Wednesday to Easter Day) in many Christian denominations, including the Dissenter congregation, the use and consumption of animal products was strictly forbidden. This meant that tallow candles could not be used and lace makers could only therefore use natural daylight to work by.

"Be the Shrovetide
High or Low,
Out the Candles
We Must Blow"[36]

The quarrymen, (often husbands of lace makers) working in the 2000 year old caves of the Beer Stone quarry, also used tallow candles to work by and consequently, they too could not work during Lent. As the quarrymen were paid by the amount of stone that was hewn, the Lent period was a poor time for the villagers. However, the loss of stone production, and consequent loss of revenue, to the Bishops of Exeter Cathedral led the Bishops to allow the use of candles in the caves, by blessing the candles on Shrove Tuesday. Would the lace maker wives have been able to use this to their advantage too?

This black and white photograph, a reproduction of an earlier photograph or postcard, hangs in the Dolphin Hotel in Beer. It is labelled "Lace Makers at Beer Circa 1900" and is possibly another "postcard" of Betsy Woodgate, working outside in the daylight. The thatched cottages no longer exist and there is only one remaining cobbled path in Beer, which is behind the old Gospel Hall.

Photo courtesy of the Clinch family of the Dolphin Hotel, Beer.

By 1840 Price's[37], the candle makers, had perfected a composite candle of refined tallow and coconut oil that burned brightly without smoke or smell. They were ready for Queen Victoria's wedding. "It was traditional for every loyal household to burn a candle in its front room window on the evening of the monarch's wedding, and in London on February 20th most people lit one of Price's new stearine 'composite' candles." It is doubtful whether the lace makers of Beer could have afforded such candles.

The newspaper, The Morning Post, of Friday 24 January 1840, describes the lace makers thus: "These poor women derive a scanty subsistence from making lace but the trade has latterly so declined that had it not been for the kind consideration of her Majesty in ordering this dress, they would have been destitute this winter. No one can form an idea of the gratitude they express who has not heard it from their own lips".

In 1848, William Augustus P. Hewett in part of his poem "The Christian muse's birth-place, and filial honour's tribute, a poem" wrote

... The low priced lace abounding from the loom,
Has withered now the lace trade's bloom,
For pillow lace is paid so small a price,
As to support the maker's can't suffice,
And either to the workhouse they must go,
Or else without, extreme distress must know....

"Reports from Commissioners 1864[38] (Examples of cubic feet of space per head at lace schools. Effects upon health)"

"219. At Mrs Driver's, Beer, Devon, a room in which eight persons worked, gave 80 cubic fee for each person.

229. The Rev C Glascott, vicar of Seaton and Beer, states "The employment is injurious to the bodily health, owing to the confinement in small close rooms with no fire-place or ventilation and the consequent impurity of the air".

The 1841 Census for the tithing of Beer shows 85 females in Beer occupied as Lace Makers and 116 in Branscombe. Whilst we don't know who exactly was employed in the making of the lace for the wedding gown, those shown on the census may well have been involved. Whilst my focus has been on Beer and Branscombe, it is highly possible that some lace makers came from further afield.

The names of people employed as Lace Makers in the 1841 census in Beer and Branscombe are shown in Appendices 2 & 3. Appendix 4 shows the 1841 population information for the Colyton Hundred, of which Beer and Branscombe formed a part.

Queen Victoria's Wedding

Queen Victoria and Prince Albert were married on 10th February 1840, at the Chapel Royal, St James's Palace and, by Royal Command, Jane attended the wedding.

The streets of London were decorated for the Royal Wedding with almost every house strewn with flags and banners. Gas light illuminations were also on show and at 76 St James Street, where Jane lived and worked, *"A crown having a star on either side, rising from a vase, and having wreaths of flowers in proper colours in variegated lamps"*[39] was on display. (Perhaps the design was based on the central section of the flounce?) In murky London what a sight it must have been!

The villagers of Beer were also celebrating[40]. Banners and flags abounded. The Beer Band played the National Anthem and officers and men from the Coast Guard service fired a Royal Salute. In the

Reenactment photograph.
Wedding dress of Queen Victoria with lace flounce and veil clearly visible.
The Royal Collection © 2010, Her Majesty Queen Elizabeth II

afternoon about 150 of the lace makers who worked on Her Majesty's Wedding dress, drank tea at the New Inn, (now the Beer Newsagents) courtesy of Jane, who had sent them £10.00 (approximately £80 in 2013's money) for the purpose.

World's New Inn.
(Now the Beer Newsagent)
Circa 1868, about 28 years
after Queen Victoria's wedding.

Photo courtesy Seaton Museum

After the Wedding

On 20th February 1840, an advertisement appeared in The Morning Post "to announce to the nobility and gentry" that Miss Bidney has for sale "an extensive variety of Court Suits, Bridal Dresses, Flounces, Berthas, Pelerines, Squares, Nets, Scarfs (sic), Cuffs and Laces of all widths."

Jane's name appeared in the newspapers again in an advertisement for Madame Tussaud's! Madame Tussaud's were to display the "Marriage Group"[41] with "Her Majesty in her nuptial dress of Honiton Point Lace, by Miss Bidney, manufacturer of the whole of the lace for Her Majesty's bridal attire …" I can't think that the actual wedding dress went on loan to Madame Tussaud's and regretfully, Madame Tussaud's cannot, currently, locate any historical documentation relating to the display.

The last "royal" entry we have for Jane is a payment to her from Queen Victoria's wardrobe accounts of £62 in 1842 (approximately £5,500 in 2013's money).

The total amount paid to Jane from 1837 to 1842 amounted to £527-8-0 (approximately £50, 000 in 2013). Newspaper reports at the time suggested that the final cost of the wedding dress was £1,000. It is likely that this was the total cost of the wedding dress, including the white Spitalfields silk of the skirt, rather than just the lace itself. Whilst we have information about how much was paid to Jane, there is no record of what was paid, by Jane, to the lace makers themselves.

On 21st November 1840, Queen Victoria and Prince Albert's first child was born; Victoria, the Princess Royal. Queen Victoria commissioned a christening robe to be made which was to be a replica of her wedding dress. This christening robe was made by Janet Sutherland but was trimmed with Honiton Lace. Was this lace also purchased from Jane? Was it made by the lace- makers of Beer? We don't know.

This christening robe was then used for all Royal Christenings until it became too fragile to wear. Prince George Alexander Louis of Cambridge (the great, great, great, great grandson of Queen Victoria) was therefore christened, on 23rd October 2013, in a replica of the original gown. This replica gown was made by Queen Elizabeth II's dressmaker Angela Kelly.

Jane's later life

On 12th May 1842, at Craven Chapel, St James, London, Jane married a widower, Nathaniel Washbourne, of Gloucester. Nathaniel was a Silk Mercer and one time Alderman and Mayor of Gloucester and we can assume that Jane met Nathaniel through her lace trade work.

Sometime following their marriage, Jane went to live with Nathaniel in Norfolk Terrace in Gloucester[42]. Perhaps, following their marriage, Jane was able to continue her lace trade via her husband's work.

From the Death Duty Register relating to Jane's father's estate, apart from the monetary value, there was no way to tell what else made up the estate. However, on the 18 May 1844[43], a legal agreement was made between Nathaniel and Jane and, a John Donelan and his wife Elizabeth, relating to a property in Beer.

It would seem that the property had been a marriage settlement upon the impending marriage of Thomas Bidney (widow) Jane's father, to Jane Loyde (widow), Jane's stepmother. The settlement transferred a freehold property (described as Muddles, in Beer) to Thomas Bidney and Jane Loyde (upon their marriage) for life. On the death of one or the other, the property was to remain with the surviving partner. On the death of the surviving partner, the property would belong to any child or children of theirs. If they died without children, the property would belong to Thomas Bidney's lawful heirs. Jane (the widow of Thomas) had use of the property during her life and as they had no children, Jane, Thomas' daughter by his first marriage, became the rightful heir to the property upon her stepmother's death.

However, the property had been leased and released and was then in the "ownership" of Henry Corbin, Surgeon of Seaton and husband of Elizabeth nee Ludlow. Upon Henry's death, in 1831, he left the property, now called "Symes" to his son Robert, also a surgeon, but Robert died in 1834, following a short illness, leaving everything he had to his mother Elizabeth. Elizabeth married John Donelan in 1835.

From copies of documents and wills, it appears that during Jane's (widow of Thomas) lifetime the property had been converted into four tenements and, Thomas' widow borrowed money from Samuel Newbery using the property as security. It also seems that when the property was assigned to Henry Corbin, it may not have been disclosed to him that the property was leasehold, rather than freehold. There then followed a legal wrangle by Nathaniel and Jane to reclaim the property.

To stop all further unpleasantness, (Elizabeth had been found guilty of actual bodily harm to another person and was sentenced to two years hard labour in Chelmsford in 1842, but was pardoned after one year. Her husband John was acquitted of the crime), including the eviction process, Nathaniel and Jane agreed to pay the Donelan's fifty pounds for the return of the property and, we can only assume that the property was legally returned to them sometime in 1844. As an aside; Henry Corbin's will underwent probate four times, and was not finally proved until 1867, some thirty six years after his death.

The Tithe map for Seaton and Beer, circa 1839, shows Henry Corbin as the landowner of six properties in Beer: A house and chapel, on the east side of the road and four other houses nearly opposite the chapel on the west side of the road. The chapel (Gospel Hall) still exists in Beer although it has been converted into a private dwelling. The four other houses one of which could have been the disputed property, (Muddles/Symes) have long since been replaced with later properties.

Nathanial and Jane stayed in Norfolk Terrace until Nathanial's death in 1861.

In 1871[44], Jane is shown on the census at 5 Richmond Terrace, Stretford, Hulme, Manchester with an Annia Davenport, a cook and a housemaid. Annia is recorded as an annuitant, single, aged 33, from Manchester, and Jane is recorded as a widow aged 68, also an annuitant. I don't know why Jane moved to Manchester, but whilst there she made the acquaintance of the Reverend James Gwyther of the Zion Chapel, Stretford Road. He and his wife, Elizabeth, were to remain her friends for the rest of her life. In fact, Elizabeth was born in Smallridge, Axminster, Devon, just over eleven miles from Beer and they would therefore have had their upbringing in Devon as well as the church in common.

Jane Washbourne nee Bidney, circa 1850
Photo originally from the collection of Mrs I Bidney Maunsell (Ida Allen's daughter)
Courtesy of Seaton Museum

In 1874[45], the Reverend James Gwyther retired and

with his wife, and daughter Mary Jane, moved to Argotti Manor (now the Conservative Club), St Mary Church in Torquay.

Jane also moved to Torquay as by 1881[46], now aged 79, she is shown as a boarder, with a Lady's maid, at 3 Belgrave Terrace in Torquay. It's quite possible that Jane moved to Torquay to be nearer her friends Elizabeth and James. The Reverend James died in 1878 and Elizabeth in 1881. In about 1879[47], one of the Reverend James and Elizabeth's sons, also James, who was a Physician and Surgeon, moved to Argotti manor and lived there with his unmarried sister, Mary Jane. Dr Gwyther was to be Jane's sole executor.

On 13 Nov 1882 in Torquay, Jane, aged 80, died of peritonitis caused by a gall bladder stone that she had had for the preceding three years, and Dr Gwyther was present at her death. I have been unable to trace where Jane was buried. As a non-conformist, she would not have been buried in a church cemetery. Records of council cemeteries at Torquay do not record her burial and many of the non-conformist records have not survived. Do you know where Jane was buried?

Dr Gwyther[48] moved to London in 1889, with his sister Mary Jane, and as well as attending St Luke's Home for the Dying and providing expert help in the movement for educating crippled (sic) children, he established Dr. James Gwyther's Boys' Club in the Beaconsfield Buildings, Caledonian Road, which, according to Mr Charles Booth[49], "achieved success of the truest kind". Dr Gwyther died in 1905 and following his death Mary Jane lived with another of her brothers Rev John Howe Gwyther, in Cheshire. She died at the age of 91.

Jane's Legacies

Jane left a comprehensive will, which had been written on 25th January 1881 and a codicil to the will, written on 1 September 1882. Appendix 5 shows a précis of the legacies that Jane made.

As well as the legacies that Jane left to individuals, which will be of interest to their descendants, Jane left three legacies of significance to Beer and to sailors.

Aggie Weston's

During the period 1881 and 1882, Jane came to be aware of the work being undertaken by Miss Agnes Weston. Agnes had previously corresponded with soldiers and sailors away from home and her interest in their welfare grew. In 1873, she visited the sailors in Devonport, with whom she had corresponded and who had been laid off. Here she met Sophia Wintz. They became good friends and fundraisers, eventually raising enough money to open a temperance hostel for sailors, outside the dockyard at Devonport. It was opened in May 1876 as the first "Sailor's Rest".

The success of the Devonport Sailor's Rest led to others being opened. Jane left a legacy of £100 (approximately £10,000 in 2013) to Agnes Weston for her to use for the establishment of or maintenance of a Sailors Rest or Sailors Boys Home.

It was Queen Victoria who allowed the use of the title The Royal Sailors' Rest, having endowed a "cabin" in Devonport.

So popular were these Sailors' rests that they were called "Aggie Weston's". Agnes was created a Dame of the British Empire in 1918 for her work with and concern for sailors.

Agnes died shortly after receiving this award, on 23 October 1918, at Devonport and was buried with full naval honours.

The Jane Washbourne Charity

Jane left £100 (approximately £10,000 in 2013) to the Congregational Church in Beer *"to be invested in such securities and upon such trusts as my executor may consider most desirable for the promoting of the prosperity of that Church and the comfort of the Minister thereof for the time being."*[50] The Jane Washbourne Charity is still (2013) administered by the Beer Congregational Chapel: Charity No: 262661-9

The Washbourne Memorial

Jane also left £100 (approximately £10,000 in 2013) to the National Lifeboat Association *"to be used towards providing a Life Boat for Beer near Seaton"*[51]. Whilst the RNLI have a record of Jane's legacy, they have no record of what the money was actually used for. However, they can confirm that no lifeboat was purchased for Beer.

The Fisherman's Light

Photo courtesy of Norman Lambert

It's probable that the RNLI gave the money to the Parish Council to decide what to do with the legacy. "The Fisherman's Light", and capstan, which is called the Washbourne Memorial was the result.

"On 14 September 1895 it was recommended that a lamp be fixed on the cliff and a new capstan and chain be provided for the fisherman of the village. By November 1895, the value of

the legacy with interest had risen to £131-13-3 and this was at the disposal of the council. On 3 March 1896, tenders were received and accepted for the sum of £100-15-6 by T Restorick (Boat builder of Beer)."[52]

The position of the light[53], on the cliff top, aligned with St Michael's church spire (which was removed in 1963). The light was used by local fisherman as a navigational aid when coming home. The mast and base have been removed and the light, shown at the top of the picture, now hangs in St Michael's church.

Very few people today, who see the capstan or the light in the church, know that it was part of a legacy from Jane Washbourne nee Bidney. Nor do they know of her lace fame. We therefore remember her here, with thanks for the help that she gave to the Lace Makers of Beer and her care for fishermen and sailors.

The capstan with the inscription on it is now above the children's play area in Beer.

Copyright ©Photos 2013 courtesy of Glyn Holford

IDA ALLEN NEE PIKE

Ida's early life

Four years after the death of Jane Washbourne, nee Bidney, and still during the reign of Queen Victoria, Ida Allen was born at "Long Chimney"[54] in Branscombe on 26 Dec 1876[55]. She was baptised in St Winifred's church on 28 Jan 1877[56]. Ida was the daughter of Emmanuel Pike (born about 1836 in Southleigh, Devon), a farmer, and Ann nee Bromfield (born about 1837 in Membury, Devon).

Ida was the youngest of seven children but two of her sisters died before she was born. Another sister died when Ida was eight years old and another when Ida was twelve and, no doubt, this was a very sad time for her.

Her siblings were: George (1867-1922), Emma (1870-1884), Ellen (1870-1888), Minnie (1872-1947) who married Edwin Hill, Mary (1874-?), and Elizabeth (1875-1875). Appendix 6 shows her family tree.

In 1881[57], the family were living at Mill (an area of) Branscombe and by 1891[58] they had moved to Seaside Farm, Branscombe.

Ida went to the Salcombe Regis school just over 2 miles from where she lived. On Sundays she would go up the tower of St Mary and St

Peter's church, in Salcombe Regis, to wind the clock. Her son Ted[59] said that she was much helped in this duty by a young boy from the village – her boyfriend!

Ida was not shown on either the 1881 or 1891 censuses as a lace maker but, under the pseudonym of "Primrose", she won fourth prize (£2-2s) in "The Girl's Own Paper" for her essay about making lace.

We do not know what year this was written but the Girls Own Paper was printed between 1880 and 1907. Ida must have used a little poetic licence when writing her essay; she says that her mother had died and she lived alone, which we know was not true as she was living with her parents and her mother did not die until 1924 and her father, not until 1931.

Although Ida may have used poetic license, she describes the work and life of a lace maker very accurately, particularly her reference to the shop "where I get things to make use of as we are not paid money there". This was called the Truck System.

"The way this worked was that the manufacturer ran a grocery and general shop. He or she then paid the lace makers either half in money and half in goods, or, very often, only in goods. Even then, the full value was not given."[60] Even though the Truck System was abolished by law in 1779, in practice it continued up to the 19th century.

She certainly knew about making lace and, her knowledge of the detrimental effect of the Truck System, upon Lace Makers, would stand her in good stead in her later life. The full article that Primrose wrote is shown at Appendix 7.

Ida was apprenticed[61] to Agland's of Seaton as a dressmaker. Her apprenticeship lasted for five years. She had to start work at 08.30 in the morning and didn't finish until 5.30pm. She walked there and back every day, approximately four miles, across county roads with no street lights.

In 1901[62], aged, 24, Ida was living with her mother and father, now a retired Farmer, at Hole House in Branscombe, and Ida was shown on the census as a Dress Maker.

Ida and Edwin Allen

George Edwin Farrant Allen was born in Cardiff in 1879; the son of William Arthur Allen (1849-?), an Engineer and Evaline, nee Good (1856-1953). His maternal family were from Beer and he was the great, great, grandson of Elizabeth Bidney (1776-1835), who was Jane Washbourne's (nee Bidney) aunt. He was 1st cousin 3 removed of Jane herself. (See Appendix 1)

George had one sister, Olive born in Cardiff in 1881, who married Harold Miles.

Sometime between 1881 and 1891, Evaline and her two children moved from Wales to live with her mother, Elizabeth, and father, Edwin, in Beer. Although on all the censuses Evaline was shown as married, her husband William was not shown. It seems that he may have been an engineer in the Navy and was therefore working away. Research has revealed no trace of what happened to him. Evaline probably came home to Beer to enjoy the companionship of her family and look after her parents who were in their 60s.

On 2 Jul 1902, at St Winifred's church in Branscombe, Ida married George Edwin Farrant Allen, then a marine engineer. (In later life, he dropped the "George" and used the name Edwin Farrant Allen.)

Following their marriage, they lived in Wales where their first two children, Roydon Farrant (b 1903) and Edwin Pike, known as Ted, (b 1907) were born. They then moved to Lyme in Dorset, where their last child, Inez Bidney (known as Binnie) was born in Trafalgar Cottage in

1908. Ida was very proud of her connection to Jane Bidney[63], but her son Ted, didn't think his sister was so amused to be given the Bidney name!

Edwin's mother lived in Beer on the west side of Main Street in a house called Hollyhocks and in 1904[64] Ida and Edwin purchased, for £80.00, the remaining 25 year lease on the property next door. It belonged to Clinton Devon Estates but was then occupied by a Miss Prescott. The property had, since the 1850s, been a Grocery shop[65].

Although notice had been given to Miss Prescott in 1904, it wasn't until 1910 that Miss Prescott finally vacated the premises and Ida and her family could take possession of it. They initially called the property Branscombe House.

Ida's son Ted[66] said that it was in the August of 1910 that the family finally moved in. The streets were dusty, with no tarmac, and there were no streetlights. Their furniture was brought in on a cart. The house had a passage running through it from the front door to the back door – leading to the Manor Yard and the outside pail toilet. Despite over the years many pleas, Ida would not allow an inside toilet to be built – she didn't believe in them! There was no running water in the house. They collected rainwater and, domestic water was drawn from the brook outside. Downstairs on the right hand side was the room used as a shop. On the left, there was a small parlour. At the back were a scullery and a lean-to kitchen. A spiral staircase led to the two bedrooms upstairs, one long and thin which was later partitioned to provide a separate room for Binnie.

Most of all Ted recalled the rats. The house was infested. They ran across the floors, they were in the roof and ran up and down inside the lathe and plaster walls. He was even bitten on his bottom, as a child, whilst asleep! The house was consequently covered in rat traps.

Ida and Edwin were well known and well thought of in Beer and when the 1911 census was issued for completion by householders themselves, Edwin was the enumerator for Beer and filled in the forms on behalf of many of the residents[67]. For example, he completed the form on behalf of Betsey Woodgate. On the 1911 census Ida was shown as a Honiton Lace Dealer.

Edwin was called up for Service with the Inland Water Transport section of the Royal Engineers in 1916 and saw active service in France. At the time of his enlistment, he was living with Ida and his three children at The Lace Shop in Beer. He was discharged in April 1919.

Edwin was a consultant mechanical engineer and is remembered as "*a very clever man. I think he's been attributed as having the first radio in Beer – that he made himself*".[68]

His son Ted, recalled that is was his father's suggestion to bring the first motor boats onto the beach.

Ida and The Old Lace Shop

Sometime between 1911 and 1916, Ida and Edwin changed their house name to The Old Lace Shop. They gave it a very distinctive shield shaped sign on a wrought iron bracket outside the shop. (A similar sign remains on the house to this day.)

Ida was known to be a fine needlewoman and dressmaker and she had been making lace, which she herself called "Needlepoint", since her teens. Her son Ted, described his mother as a brilliant business woman[69]. It is hardly surprising then, that with her knowledge of lace and lace making, that she set up the lace shop. We know that Ida continued to make lace herself but was reliant on the lace workers of

Beer and Branscombe to make the lace that she would sell in her shop. Some people in Branscombe remember their relatives taking their lace to Mrs Allen for sale. She "had a keen eye like a hawk and she could pick out the little mistakes".[70]

On the 1911 census for Branscombe there were seventy-eight people whose occupations were associated with the lace industry, forty-eight of whom described themselves as lace makers or workers. Only eighteen described themselves as Honiton Lace makers and nine Point Lace menders/workers.[71] Two were dealers in lace and one a lace manufacturer. (See Appendix 8)

In Beer however, whilst individuals described their lace occupations similarly, the enumerator annotated the occupation entries to be more specific. Thanks to Ida's husband Edwin, who was the enumerator, we know that: thirty-three people were Honiton Lace makers/workers, four (including Ida) were dealers in lace, one was a point lace worker,[72] one was as a designer of lace and one was a lace instructor[73]. In addition, eight old age pensioners were former Honiton Lace makers and twelve were Plain Nottingham Net Lace workers/menders.[74] (See Appendix 9)

Over 100 people worked for Ida,[75] including boys - Ted mentioned specifically Percy Westlake. Dorothy Mutter (1891-1978) who married Gerald Restorick (1891-1969) in 1918 worked directly for Ida on the lace and Doris Perkins (1905–1963) was an apprentice.

The earliest photograph we can currently find referring directly to Ida and the Lace Shop is a picture postcard circ 1914, taken outside her shop, of a lace tunic and a lace maker.

Although the writing is virtually illegible, what can be read reads: "Honiton Tunic" Designed and made under the direction of Mrs Allen. Regretfully, no name is given of the lace maker herself. Do you know who she was?

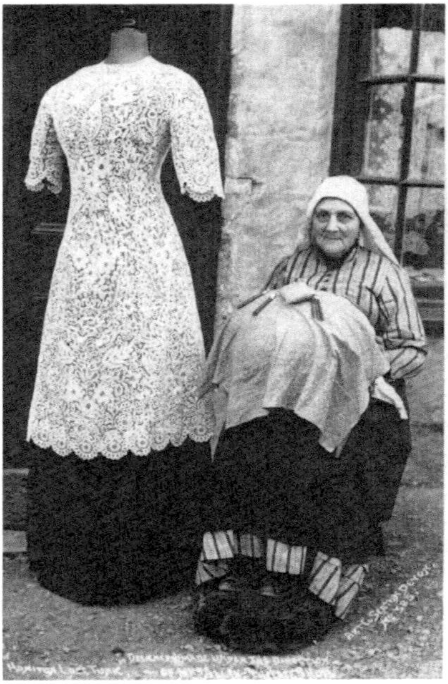

Lace Tunic and the Lace Maker
Photo courtesy of Seaton Museum

In 1926,[76] the lease on The Lace Shop was starting to expire and Clinton Devon Estates would not renew the lease. However, for a rent of £1 a week, they agreed that major improvements could be carried out. The floors were renewed and finally, the source of the rat problem was discovered – a hole directly from a sewer was found. This was filled with masses of broken glass and closed. A lathe and plaster wall was taken down, that had rotted, which dropped the upstairs floor by two to three inches! Ida still would not have an indoor toilet or a bathroom. A new kitchen with a flat roof designed by Edwin was, however, installed as was running water.

As well as selling lace, Ida was an Agent for John White RI (a member of the Royal Institute of Painters in water colours & ROI (a member of the Royal Institute of painters in oil colours). She also sold some antiques from her shop too.

This photograph, looking up Fore Street, from the 1920's, shows The Old Lace shop on the left hand side with its distinctive shield shaped shop sign. The gate to Hollyhocks, on the left of the lace shop, can just be seen.

Photo courtesy of Seaton Museum

Looking towards The Lace Shop today.

Continuing the Royal Patronage

Ida's lace was sent all over the world. She designed lace, was a judge of lace making and also sold her lace to the Chicks of Branscombe who were a well known lace manufacturing family.

Such was the trust in Ida and her lace workers that Queen Mary (1867-1953), the wife of George V (1865-1936) grandson of Queen Victoria, [77]sent old lace from her collection to Ida to be cleaned and repaired. She used old fashioned methods and was very proficient at cleaning lace[78]. She wrapped the lace around a jar and used a mixture of chloride and spirits of salts. If during the lace making process a lace maker pricked her finger and left blood on the lace, she would remove the blood with gin.

From newspaper reports[79] we also know that Princess Marie Louise (1872 -1956), who was the last Granddaughter of Queen Victoria, visited Ida's shop several times. Princess Marie Louise had told her uncle The Duke of Connaught – (1850–1942), who was Prince Arthur, the third son of Queen Victoria, about Ida's shop and, in 1932[80] he spent some time there, talking to her about the lace that his mother wore and purchasing several pieces of lace himself.

In 1932, Princess Mary, (Victoria Alexandra Alice Mary, Viscountess Lascelles), (1897-1965) the third child and only daughter of King George V and Queen Mary, was presented with a wedding gift of a lace collar, made under Ida's supervision. The lace collar was paid for by every woman in Beer named Mary. The collar was taken to Buckingham Palace by the then vicar's wife, Mrs Mary Hollis.

The Lord Chamberlain[81] on a visit to the shop with Daisy Greville, the Countess of Warwick, recommended to Ida that she should hold a Royal Warrant. Ida was initially very happy to do so until she found out that it would cost 100 guineas (£100-100 shillings) per year! Ida therefore had a very distinctive envelope printed for use in her lace shop. Whilst not bearing the "By Appointment" crown, there is no doubt that Ida was proud of the royal patronage given to her.

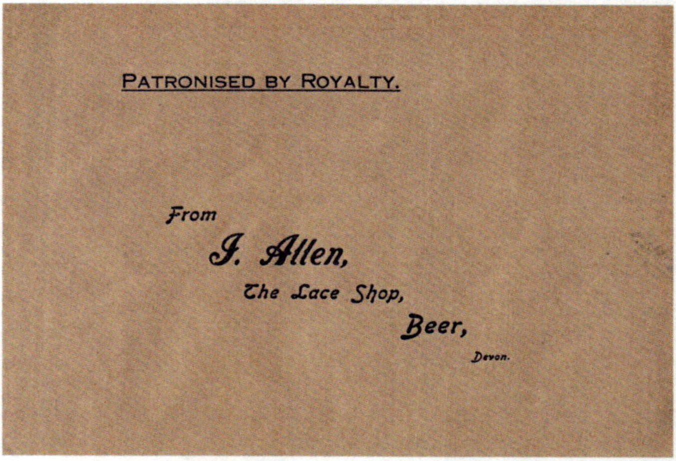

This A6 (10x 8" /25.5x18 cm) envelope, is from the collection of, and is reproduced courtesy of, G Holford

Queen Elizabeth II, when she embarked on a tour of Canada and the United States of America in May 1939,[82] took with her a handkerchief edged with lace with roses and thistles in the design, made by Ida and her lace workers. It seems that the handkerchief was part of a selection ordered by Queen Elizabeth. Lady Helen Graham, Lady-in-waiting to the Queen conveyed the message to Ida "*The Queen directs me to say that she has greatly admired these specimens of lace and is deeply interested to know that this beautiful handcraft is still carried on by Devonshire workers as in the past*".[83]

Other notable visitors to Ida's shop included:[84]

Winston Churchill in about 1929;

Dwight D Eisenhower, (the 34th President of the United States and Supreme Commander of the Allied Forces during World War II) visited in 1944 – probably as part of a visit to Beer Quarry Caves which were being used to house munitions for D Day as well as visiting other USA forces in the area;

Bernard Montgomery, 1st Viscount Montgomery of Alamein;

Douglas Hogg 1st Viscount Hailsham, and

Freddie Mills the world light heavyweight champion from 1948 to 1950.

Ida Allen outside her lace shop. (Date not known.)

Photo courtesy of Seaton Museum

Lace Manufacturing in Beer Comes to an End

In 1934, Ida wrote to the Devonshire Association for the Advancement of Science, Literature and Art, saying that lace making was dying out; her oldest worker being ninety-seven years of age although still making beautiful lace. Regretfully, Ida did not say who this lace maker was. She went on to say that the young were not taking up the art of lace making.

Ida's husband died of pneumonia in 1936, a relatively young man of fifty seven years, and was buried in St Winifred's Church in Branscombe. Ida continued working in the shop after his death.

She moved to Seaton, to live with her daughter, in the mid 1950s, where she died of cancer, aged eighty-two, in 1959. She was buried with her husband in St Winifred's Church in Branscombe.

Ida left her lace collection to her daughter Binnie, who very generously gave pieces of the lace to her godson's (Glyn Holford) mother as birthday and Christmas gifts. Pieces of this precious lace still have their original blue paper backing. Glyn remembers seeing Mrs Allen in her Lace Shop and recalls her as a small elderly round lady, with white hair, dressed in black.

A Piece of Beer Lace from the collection of Glyn Holford

And Now?

In 1981, Princess Marguerita of Yugoslavia (1932- 2013) commissioned the Beer Lace Makers to create a piece of lace as her wedding gift to Prince Charles and Princess Diana (Lady Diana Spencer 1961-1977). David Skipp designed the motif which combined the Prince of Wales feathers with part of the Spencer crest.

In 1982, for the christening of Prince William, the Beer Lace Makers made a book of lace Nursery Rhymes, from designs by David Skipp and Judith Green. The book was presented by May Wakley, a lace maker and resident of Beer, at Buckingham Palace. Unlike previous royal designs, these were not destroyed but are held in the Exeter Museum.

Also in 1982, as part of the Axe Valley Maritime Exhibition, Queen Victoria's Wedding dress flounce was temporarily returned to Beer and exhibited in St Michael's Church. It was transported from London under Police escort and pairs of villagers slept in the church overnight to protect it. Were you one of the villagers?

Lace making continues in Beer, but as a pastime and not as an industry. The lace makers, having been taught, have become teachers themselves and classes are still held fortnightly in the Beer Congregational Hall. The Beer Lace Group still produce the most exquisite pieces of delicate lace, often for commemorative purposes.

Piece produced to mark the 100th anniversary of the start of World War I

In all my research, one of the saddest things has been that I have rarely found the names of the lace makers to be able to attribute them to these historic pieces of Beer Lace. Did one of your ancestors work on these pieces of lace? Do you work on them now? For future generations, it would be worthy to record their names. Please, do let me know.

ACKNOWLEDGEMENTS

My first thanks must go to Lynn Squire as without her knowledge, experience and patient tutelage I would not have embarked on the route of genealogy. Consequently, I would not have discovered the joys of finding history hidden in plain sight.

My gratitude goes to Kim Pooley and Rob Shepherd for their precious time, encouragement and feedback.

I am indebted to the following for their time and assistance in providing me with information during my research:
Julie Crocker, Assistant Archivist at The Royal Archives, Windsor Castle;
Peter Moorman, Assistant Librarian, R.N.L.I.;
Madame Tussaud's;
Norman Lambert;
Trish and Brain McMahon and,
The staff at Devon Heritage Services.

My thanks also go to the following for their kind permission to publish material:
Dover Publications on behalf of Pat Earnshaw; Costume – the journal of the Costume Society;
Price's Patent Candles Ltd;
Alan Rosevear of Turnpikes.org.uk;
Ted Gosling on behalf of Seaton Museum;
Norman Lambert;
Carol McFadzean and Elizabeth Trebble of Devon Lace Teachers;
Branscombe Parish Council;
Barbara Farquharson and Joan Doern of The Branscombe Project;
Richard Scott and the Beer Lace Group; and The Clinch family of the Dolphin Hotel, Beer.

I also acknowledge the following sources used in my research:
Devon Heritage Services;
Census data under Open Government Licence, Original data: Census Returns of England and Wales, Kew, Surrey, England;
The National Archives of the UK (TNA);
Public Record Office (PRO);
Leeds District Probate Registry;
General Register Office (GRO);
London Metropolitan Archives;
British Newspaper Archive;
Dictionary of Victorian Painters by Christopher Wood 2nd Edition ISBN 0 902028 72 3
University of Essex – Historical online population reports;
The Official Website of the British Monarchy, Queen Victoria Diamond Jubilee Scrapbook 1897;
The Branscombe Lace Makers edited by Barbara Farquharson and Joan Doern;
A History of Prices Candles;
The Branscombe Project;
Royal Naval Museum Library;
Britain in Old Photographs – Beer - Norman Lambert and Ted Gosling ISBN 978 0 7524 6190 8;
Beer Tithe Map and apportionments and,
John Scott of Beer Quarry Caves.

Finally, and most importantly, my heartfelt gratitude goes to Glyn Holford for his unwavering support and encouragement and, for sharing his heritage with me.

Endnotes

1. Seaton and Beer Parish Records
2. Hannah may have been baptised on 26 October 1780 in the New Meeting House, Honiton on Otter, but her name was recorded as Anna Maria Newberry. (The writing of names in Parish registers at that time was haphazard; the clergymen often recording names as they thought they heard them. Hence first names were miss-recorded and the spelling of family names often changed).
3. Seaton and Beer Parish Records
4. English Dissenters were Christians who separated from the Church of England in the 16th, 17th and 18th centuries. They originally agitated for a wide-reaching Protestant Reformation of the Established Church, and triumphed briefly under Oliver Cromwell. King James I of England, VI of Scotland had said "no bishop, no king" Cromwell capitalised on that phrase, abolishing both upon founding the Commonwealth of England. After the restoration of the monarchy in 1660, the episcopacy was reinstalled and the rights of the Dissenters were limited: the Act of Uniformity 1662 required Anglican ordination for all clergy, and many instead withdrew from the state church. These ministers and their followers came to be known as Nonconformists, though originally this term referred to refusal to use certain vestments and ceremonies of the Church of England, rather than separation from it. Dissenters opposed state interference in religious matters, and founded their own churches, educational establishments, and communities; some emigrated to The New World. The early congregationalists were called separatists or independents to distinguish them from the similarly Calvinistic Presbyterians. Each congregation

independently and autonomously runs its own affairs. Some congregationalists in Britain still call themselves Independent.

5. The Evangelical Magazine 1856 - from newspaper articles retrieved by Mandy Pemberton from Australia in Sept 2010
6. Mary, Hannah and Thomas were buried in St Gregory's Church graveyard in Seaton. (Information from Parish Registers)
7. Seaton and Beer Parish Records
8. Seaton and Beer Parish Records
9. Richard Loyde's first wife Mary was buried on 30th July 1776 (Seaton and Beer Parish records)
10. Mary, Hannah and Thomas were buried in St Gregory's Church graveyard in Seaton. (Information from Parish Registers)
11. There is no current trace of Thomas' original Will. The information has been obtained from the National Archive Death Duty Register of 1806
12. It seems that Probate and Tax were recorded in whole pounds to the nearest £50. Thomas' estate was therefore likely to have been between £750 and £800
13. 1841 Census Data. This was the first census to record all names in a household, their age, whether they were male or female, their occupations and whether or not they were born in the county where the census took place. For the tithing of Beer, only the street name was recorded – no house names or numbers. In 1841, her step mother was living on independent means, in Main Street. Mary Searle, a Lace Maker was living in the same household
14. Information from a recording made by Ted Allen, in 1978, courtesy of Norman Lambert
15. Records of Sun Life Fire Office 1834: Insured Jane Bidney. Held at the London Metropolitan Archives
16. Records of Sun Life Fire Office 1837: Insured Jane Bidney. Held at the London Metropolitan Archives
17. Register of Shipping 1786-1811. Devon Records Office DSR/EXE/1/1 32895/1
18. Jack Rattenbury: fisherman, pilot, seaman and smuggler 1778-1844.

19. From research carried out by Dr H J Yallop, who was curator of the Honiton Allhallows Museum. In 1992 he published an account of "The history of the Honiton Lace Making Industry".
20. A Dictionary of Lace, Pat Earnshaw. Dover Publications Inc. ISBN 13: 9780486404820, ISBN 10: 048640482X
21. Advert from The Morning Post, London, 20th February 1840.
22. Seaton and Beer Parish Records
23. Dorset, England, Dorchester Prison Admission and Discharge Registers, 1782-1901 Prisoner Register 1812-1827. As an alternative to imprisonment, those convicted of smuggling were often enrolled in The Navy
24. Seaton and Beer Parish Records
25. The 1841 census was the first census to record names and occupations of household residents. It was usual for only the occupation of the Head of the household to be recorded; however, there are numerous other instances where the occupations of all the residents were recorded.
26. Information taken from a postcard of Mrs Woodgate which includes letters from Buckingham Palace
27. The Official Website of the British Monarchy
28. Queen Victoria Diamond Jubilee Scrapbook 1897 on-line
29. Morning Post (24 Jan 1840), The Examiner (09 Feb 1840), Queen Victoria's Wedding by Angela Magnotti Andrews.
30. The Examiner, London, Sunday 9th February 1840
31. The Morning Post Friday 24th January 1840
32. William Dyce. Dictionary of Victorian Painters by Christopher Wood
33. Sir Henry Cole (1808 – 1882); Played a key role in the introduction of the Penny Post, and is sometimes credited with the design of the world's first postage stamp, the Penny Black. He is also credited with devising the concept of sending greetings cards at Christmas time, introducing the world's first commercial Christmas card in 1843. Cole was instrumental in the development of the Royal College of Art as a postgraduate design school – presumably, how he met William Dyce.

34. Extract from William Dyce's letter to Sir Henry Cole of 18 June 1852, quoted in Kay Staniland and Santina M Levey, 'Queen Victoria's Wedding Dress and Lace', Costume, 17 (1983).
35. Myles Birket Foster (1825-1899) RWS. Dictionary of Victorian Painters by Christopher Wood
36. "Shrovetide" the period usually of three days immediately preceding Ash Wednesday. This saying, of unknown origin, was related to me by John Scott of Beer Quarry Caves, together with the information about the dispensation granted by the Bishops of Exeter.
37. A History of Price's Candles Courtesy of Price's Patent Candles Ltd
38. From extracts from old newspapers put together from newspaper articles retrieved by Mandy Pemberton from Australia in Sept 2010
39. London Standard Tuesday 11th February 1840
40. Exeter and Plymouth Gazette Saturday 15th February 1840
41. The Morning Chronicle Wednesday July 1st 1840
42. The 1851 Census shows Jane and Nathaniel, living with two servants
43. Courtesy of Norman Lambert
44. The 1871 Census
45. One of the books for the Belgrave Congregational Church, Torquay, (Devon Records Office ref 5471D/1) shows that The Reverend James Gwyther, his wife and daughter were members of the church from November 1874.
46. The 1881 Census
47. One of the books for the Belgrave Congregational Church, Torquay, (Devon Records Office ref 5471D/1) shows that Dr James Gwyther was a member of the church from February 1879.
48. Obituary of Dr James Gwyther, The Times 1905
49. Charles James Booth (1840 – 1916) was an English philanthropist and social researcher. He is most famed for his innovative work on documenting working class life in London at the end of the 19th century

50. From the Will of Jane Washbourne
51. From the Will of Jane Washbourne
52. Norman Lambert
53. Britain in Old Photographs: Beer, Norman Lambert and Ted Gosling. The History Press ISBN 978 0 7524 6190 8
54. Information from a recording made by Ted Allen, in 1978, courtesy of Norman Lambert
55. Branscombe Parish Records
56. Branscombe Parish Records
57. 1881 Census
58. 1891 Census
59. Information from a recording made by Ted Allen, in 1978, courtesy of Norman Lambert
60. "The Branscombe Lace Makers" edited by Barbara Farquharson and Joan Doern
61. Information from a recording made by Ted Allen, in 1978, courtesy of Norman Lambert
62. 1901 Census
63. Information from a recording made by Ted Allen, in 1978, courtesy of Norman Lambert
64. Information from a recording made by Ted Allen, in 1978, courtesy of Norman Lambert
65. From Census data: The Grocers were; Susanna Wood (1851), Amy Orley, Susanna's sister in law (1861, 1871) and Sarah Leyman (1881, 1891, 1901). Sarah Leyman was Amy Orley's niece or cousin.
66. Information from a recording made by Ted Allen, in 1978, courtesy of Norman Lambert
67. The 1911 census was the first census where householders were to complete the forms themselves. Prior to this they had been completed by an enumerator (A person appointed to issue, complete, and collect census forms)
68. Edwin Purchase of Branscombe (Ida's nephew) recalling Ida's husband in "The Branscombe Lace-Makers", edited by Barbara Farquharson and Joan Doern

69. Information from a recording made by Ted Allen, in 1978, courtesy of Norman Lambert
70. Lesley Collier of Branscombe, recalling Ida Allen in "The Branscombe Lace-Makers", edited by Barbara Farquharson and Joan Doern
71. Needlepoint lace: made with a needle rather than bobbins
72. Thomas William Hammond (1853-1935) He won awards for his Nottingham Lace Designs and is known as an Artist using mainly pastels and charcoals
73. Sarah Jane Newton nee Perry (1860-1929)
74. Nottingham Plain Net: machine made lace
75. Information from a recording made by Ted Allen, in 1978, courtesy of Norman Lambert
76. Information from a recording made by Ted Allen, in 1978, courtesy of Norman Lambert
77. Western Morning News 10 February 1940
78. Information from a recording made by Ted Allen, in 1978, courtesy of Norman Lambert
79. Western Morning News 10 February 1940
80. Western Daily Press 29 November 1932, Western Morning News 10 May 1939
81. Information from a recording made by Ted Allen, in 1978, courtesy of Norman Lambert
82. Western Morning News 19 May 1939
83. Arizona Periodical July 1979
84. Information from a recording made by Ted Allen, in 1978, courtesy of Norman Lambert.

APPENDICES

APPENDIX 1
Bidney Family Tree

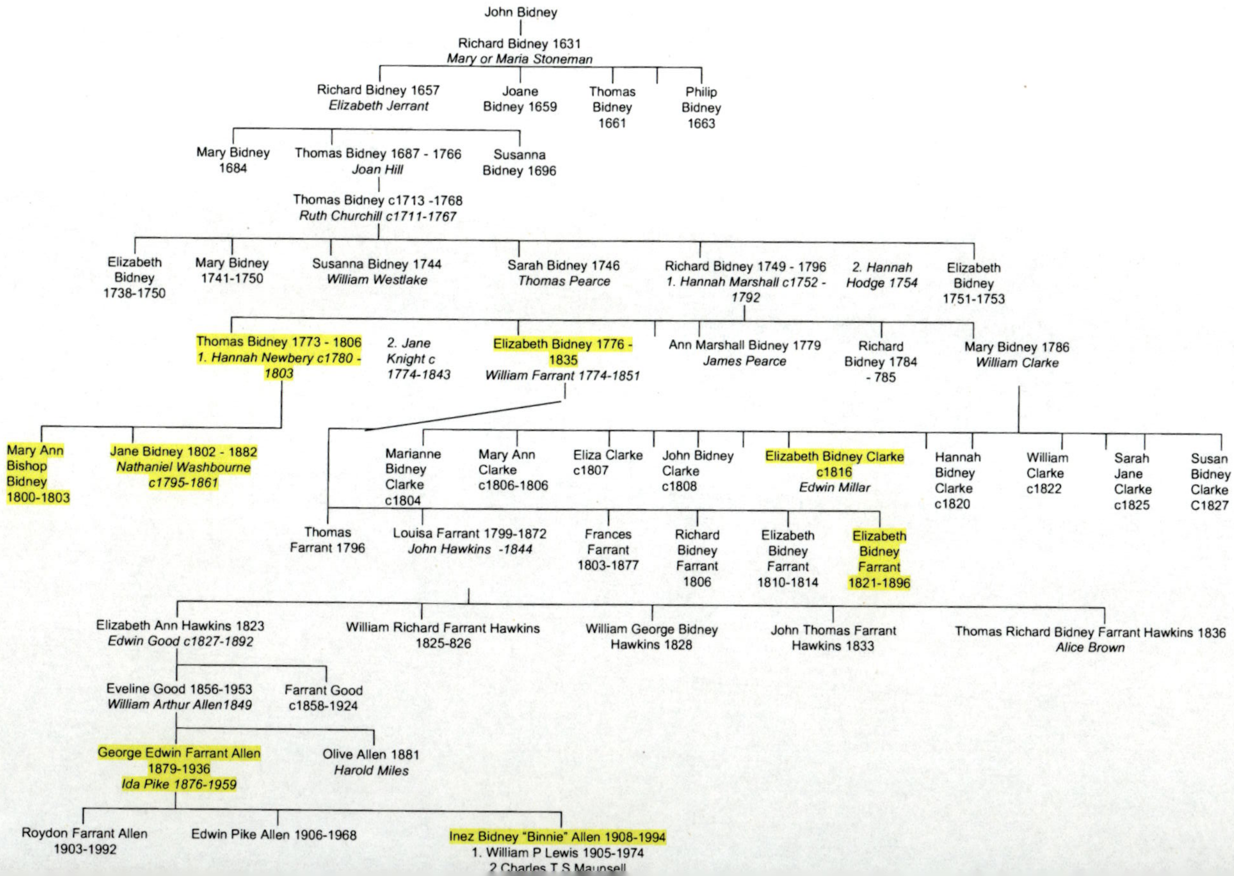

APPENDIX 2

Names of Lace Makers From the Beer 1841 Census						
	First Name	Surname	Age	Born Circa	Occupation	Address
1	Mary	Abbot	15	1826	Lace Maker	Main Street
2	Joan	Bartlett	35	1806	Lace M	Beer Street
3	Maria	Bartlett	40	1801	Lace M	Broad ?
4	Sarah	Butter	45	1796	Lace M	Beer Street
5	Elizabeth	Butter	35	1806	Lace M	Beer Street
6	Hannah	Butter	35	1806	Lace M	Cross
7	Mary Ann	Butter	15	1826	Lace M	Beer Street
8	Sarah	Caddy	90	1751	Lace Maker	Main Street
9	Elizabeth	Cawley	60	1781	Lace Maker	Main Street
10	Emma	Copp	35	1806	Lace Maker	Main Street
11	Mary	Cox	25	1816	Lace Maker	Main Street
12	Henrietta	Cumbden (?)	16	1825	Lace Maker	Main Street
13	Eliza	Driver	40	1801	Lace M	Chapel Lane
14	Mary	Driver	60	1781	Lace M	Beer Street
15	Louisa	Driver	20	1821	Lace Maker	Main Street
16	Martha	Gaskin (?)	40	1801	Lace M	Illegible
17	Ann	Gibb	25	1816	Lace M	Beer Street
18	Mary	Gibb	55	1786	Lace M	Beer Street
19	Susanna	Gibb (?)	65	1776	Lace M	Illegible
20	Sarah	Gibble (?)	20	1821	Lace M	Beer Street
21	Pricilla	Gibbs	43	1798	Lace M	Illegible
22	Eliza	Good	10	1831	Lace M	Beer Street
23	Jane	Ham	65	1776	Lace Maker	Berry Lane
24	Mary	Hardick (?)	30	1811	Lace M	Beer Street
25	Mary	Hare (?)	16	1825	Lace Maker	Main Street
26	Sarah	Hare (?)	15	1826	Lace M	Beer Street
27	Tamzin	Hayman	50	1791	Lace Maker	Chapel Hill
28	Ann	Horsford	45	1796	Lace Maker	Longhill
29	Elizabeth	Howard	30	1811	Lace M	Illegible
30	Jane	Jenkins	20	1821	Lace Maker	Chapel Hill
31	Illegible	Johnson (?)	15	1826	Lace M	Beer Street

32	Hannah	King (?)	25	1816	Lace M	Stoke Lane (?)
33	Alice	Lockyer	40	1801	Lace Maker	Main Street
34	Anna	Marshall or Marchant	40	1801	Lace M	Illegible
35	Eliza	Marshall or Marchant	20	1821	Lace M	Illegible
36	Betsy	Marshall	70	1771	Lace Maker	Main Street
37	Matilda	Miller	25	1916	Lace Maker	Main Street
38	Ann	Miller	12	1826	Lace Maker	Main Street
39	Ann	Miller	20	1821	Lace M	Cross
40	Ann	Miller	35	1806	Lace M	Beer Street
41	Mary	Mills	15	1826	Lace M	Caddys Row
42	Susan	Mills	10	1831	Lace Maker	Main Street
43	Annie	Mutter	20	1821	Lace Maker	Main Street
44	Anna	Newton	20	1821	Lace M	Beer Street
45	Elizth	Newton	15	1826	Lace M	Green Lanes (?)
46	Mary	Newton	70	1771	Lace M	Illegible
47	Patience	Newton	20	1821	Lace M	Green Lanes (?)
48	Sarah	Newton See Note A	40	1801	Lace Maker	Main Street
49	Maria	Pearce	45	1796	Lace Maker	Berry Hill
50	Elizabeth	Pearce	10	1831	Lace Maker	Berry Hill
51	Herzia (?)	Perry	25	1813	Lace M	Beer Street
52	Harriet	Pine	33	1808	Lace Maker	Main Street
53	Sarah	Potter (?)	25	1816	Lace M	Beer Street
54	Mary	Rafael	30	1811	Lace M	Caddys Row
55	Caroline (?)	Restorick (?)	35	1806	Lace M	Cross
56	Elizabeth	Robertson	50	1791	Lace Maker	Main Street
57	Mary or Fanny	Roddenbury (?)	30	1811	Lace M	Illegible
58	Mary Ann	Roddenbury (?)	20	1821	Lace M	Illegible
59	Susan	Row	25	1816	Lace M	Illegible

60	Mary	Rowe	20	1821	Lace Maker	Longhill
61	Elizabeth	Rutter	20	1821	Lace Maker	Caddys Row
62	Elizabeth	Searle	30	1811	Lace Maker	Longhill
63	Martha	Searle	20	1821	Lace Maker	Main Street
64	Mary	Searle	35	1806	Lace Maker	Main Street
65	Mary	Seaward	20	1821	Lace M	Beer Street
66	Mary	Seaward	33	1808	Lace Maker	Chapel Hill
67	Elizabeth	Seaward	10	1831	Lace Maker	Chapel Hill
68	Gemima	Seaward	30	1811	Lace M	Beer Street
69	Hannah	Seaward	40	1801	Lace M	Chapel Hill
70	Keziah	Seaward	30	1811	Lace M	Beer Street
71	Elizabeth	Smale	14	1827	Lace Maker	Main Street
72	Sarah	Smith	60	1781	Lace M	Illegible
73	Ann	Smith	35	1806	Lace M	Illegible
74	Elizabeth	Starling (?)	20	1821	Lace Maker	Main Street
75	Elizabeth	Starling (?)	16	1825	Lace Maker	Main Street
76	Fanny	Starling (?)	13	1828	Lace Maker	Main Street
77	Mary	Sutton (?)	60	1781	Lace M	Beer Street
78	Lydia	Stokes	40	1801	Lace Maker	Main Street
79	Ann	Waldron	15	1826	Lace Maker	Longhill
80	Jeanna	Westlake	20	1821	Lace Maker	Chapel Hill
81	Mary Ann	White	30	1811	Lace M	Beer Street
82	Mary	Williams	33	1808	Lace Maker	Chapel Hill
83	Lydia	Woodgate (See note B)	20	1821	Lace M	Broad Street (?)
84	Sarah	Woodgate (See note C)	60	1781	Lace M	Chapel Lane
85	Elizabeth	Illegible	45	1796	Lace M	Beer Street

Notes:

A. Sarah Newton was the mother of Betsy Woodgate (Elizabeth Ann nee Newton)

B. The surname Woodgate has been transcribed as Woodcate in some transcriptions of the census

C. The surname Woodgate has been transcribed as Woodcock in some transcriptions of the census

APPENDIX 3

Names of Lace Makers From the Branscombe 1841 Census						
	First Name	Surname	Age	Born Circa	Occupation	Address
1	Ann	Agland	13	1828	Lace Maker	Goosemoor
2	Charlotte	Abbott	20	1821	Lace Maker	Dean
3	Ann	Bartlett	50	1791	Lace Maker	Mill
4	Elizabeth	Bartlett	15	1826	Lace Maker	Goosemoor
5	Elizabeth	Bartlett	19	1822	Lace Maker	Little Seaside
6	Jane	Bartlett	15	1826	Lace Maker	Dean
7	Maryann	Bartlett	21	1820	Lace Maker	Dean
8	Sarah	Bartlett	11	1830	Lace Maker	Goosemoor
9	Sarah	Bartlett	65	1776	Lace Maker	Higher Cotte
10	Sarah	Bartlett	30	1811	Lace Maker	Dean
11	Susan	Bartlett	21	1820	Lace Maker	nr the Church
12	Maryann	Buckenhole	29	1812	Lace Maker	Dean
13	Elizabeth	Bucknel	37	1804	Lace Maker	Coast Guard Cottages
14	Elizabeth	Bucknel	20	1821	Lace Maker	Goosemoor
15	Mary	Bucknel	78	1763	Lace Maker	nr the Church
16	Louisa	Clark	34	1807	Lace Maker	Dean
17	Maryann	Clark	16	1825	Lace Maker	Dean
18	Ann	Collier	9	1832	Lace Maker	Vicarage
19	Eliza	Collier	19	1822	Lace Maker	Higher Watercombe
20	Susan	Collier	17	1824	Lace Maker	Higher Watercombe
21	Martha	Cox	17	1824	Lace Maker	Cotte
22	Mary	Cox	40	1801	Lace Maker	Cotte
23	Amy	Dowell	58	1783	Lace Maker	Vicarage
24	Any	Dowell	16	1825	Lace Maker	Vicarage
25	Elizabeth	Dowell	21	1820	Lace Maker	Vicarage
26	Elizabeth	Dowell	40	1801	Lace Maker	Vicarage
27	Elizabeth	Dowell	16	1825	Lace Maker	Vicarage
28	Emma	Dowell	13	1828	Lace Maker	Vicarage
29	Hannah	Dowell	18	1823	Lace Maker	Lower Dean
30	Isabella	Dowell	19	1822	Lace Maker	Vicarage
31	Prudence	Dowell	41	1800	Lace Maker	Vicarage

32	Rachel	Dowell	25	1816	Lace Maker	Banks
33	Maryann	Dyer	27	1814	Lace Maker	Dean
34	Lydia	Eveleigh	55	1786	Lace Maker	Vicarage
35	Mary	Eveleigh	27	1814	Lace Maker	Vicarage
36	Elizabeth	French	20	1821	Lace Maker	nr the Church
37	Elizabeth	French	11	1830	Lace Maker	Castle
38	Sarah	French	20	1821	Lace Maker	nr the Church
39	Sarah	French	32	1809	Lace Maker	Castle
40	Mary	Gay	53	1788	Lace Maker	Vicarage
41	Mary	Gay	17	1824	Lace Maker	Vicarage
42	Ann	Gibbs	50	1791	Lace Maker	Vicarage
43	Elizabeth	Gibbs	78	1763	Lace Maker	Vicarage
44	Jane	Gill	13	1828	Lace Maker	Dean
45	Joanna	Gill	57	1784	Lace Maker	Dean
46	Susan	Gill	33	1808	Lace Maker	Vicarage
47	Rachel	Goldsworthy	23	1818	Lace Maker	Deems
48	Sarah	Green	33	1808	Lace Maker	Vicarage
49	Ann	Gush	18	1823	Lace Maker	Vicarage
50	Grace	Gush	42	1799	Lace Maker	Vicarage
51	Mary	Gush	39	1802	Lace Maker	Vicarage
52	Maryann	Gush	30	1811	Lace Maker	Dean
53	Mary Ann	Halse	30	1811	Lace Maker	nr the Church
54	Robert	Harding	13	1828	Lace Maker	Great Seaside
55	Charlotte	Hardy	40	1801	Lace Maker	Vicarage
56	Charlotte	Lockyer	26	1815	Lace Maker	Vicarage
57	Emma	Lockyer	13	1828	Lace Maker	Vicarage
58	Rachael	Lockyer	20	1821	Lace Maker	Vicarage
59	Sarah	Lockyer	11	1830	Lace Maker	Vicarage
60	Ann	Loveridge	35	1808	Lace Maker	Goosemoor
61	Jane	Lugg	38	1803	Lace Maker	Vicarage
62	Ann	Maeer	34	1807	Lace Maker	Vicarage
63	Susanna	Manly	30	1811	Lace Maker	Lower Watercombe
64	Emiline	Minify	17	1824	Lace Maker	Dean
65	Sarah	Minify	30	1811	Lace Maker	Dean
66	Elizabeth	Nevins (?)	45	1796	Lace Maker	Lower Dean
67	Sarah	Nevins (?)	16	1825	Lace Maker	Lower Dean
68	Mary	Nevins (?)	34	1807	Lace Maker	Dean
69	Amelia	Newton	23	1818	Lace Maker	Vicarage

70	Elizabeth	Newton	13	1828	Lace Maker	Millers
71	Elizabeth	Newton	21	1820	Lace Maker	Vicarage
72	Jane	Newton	18	1823	Lace Maker	Vicarage
73	Mary Ann	Norman	15	1826	Lace Maker	nr the Church
74	Ann	Northcott	40	1801	Lace Maker	Vicarage
75	Matilda	Northcott	10	1831	Lace Maker	Vicarage
76	Rhoda	Northcott	25	1816	Lace Maker	Vicarage
77	Sarah B	Northcott	30	1811	Lace Maker	nr the Church
78	Mary	Otten	45	1796	Lace Maker	nr the Church
79	Elizabeth	Otten	20	1821	Lace Maker	Bridge
80	Catherine	Parrett	25	1816	Lace Maker	nr the Church
81	Harriot	Payton	25	1816	Lace Maker	Banks
82	Ann	Perry	46	1795	Lace Maker	Vicarage
83	Mary	Perry	27	1814	Lace Maker	Vicarage
84	Mary	Perry	16	1825	Lace Maker	Castle
85	Susan	Perry	49	1792	Lace Maker	Castle
86	Caroline	Perryman	25	1816	Lace Maker	Sellerswood
87	Eliza	Perryman	24	1817	Lace Maker	nr the Church
88	Sarah	Perryman	30	1811	Lace Maker	Dean
89	Elizabeth	Pile	10	1831	Lace Maker	Little Seaside
90	Sarah	Pile	35	1806	Lace Maker	Little Seaside
91	Elizabeth	Randle	50	1791	Lace Maker	Millers
92	Elizabeth	Randle	15	1826	Lace Maker	Millers
93	Sarah	Randle	23	1818	Lace Maker	Millers
94	Sarah	Raphel	45	1796	Lace Maker	Millers
95	Ann	Richards	45	1796	Lace Maker	Vicarage
96	Mary	Rowland	45	1796	Lace Maker	Dean
97	Sarah	Sellers	17	1824	Lace Maker	Cotte
98	Hannah	Selway	25	1816	Lace Maker	Pitt
99	Elizabeth	Stevens	16	1825	Lace Maker	Vicarage
100	Emma	Stevens	10	1831	Lace Maker	Vicarage
101	Mary	Stevens	24	1817	Lace Maker	Vicarage
102	Priscilla	Stevens	25	1816	Lace Maker	nr the Church
103	Sophia	Stevens	13	1828	Lace Maker	Vicarage
104	Susan Ann	Stevens	5	1836	Lace Maker	nr the Church
105	Alice	Strong	65	1776	Lace Maker	Banks
106	Alice	Strong	30	1811	Lace Maker	Banks
107	Mary	Strong	25	1816	Lace Maker	Banks
108	Elizabeth	Summers	29	1812	Lace Maker	Little Seaside

109	Ann	Tucker	44	1797	Lace Maker	nr the Church
110	Ann	Tucker	70	1771	Lace Maker	nr the Church
111	Eliza	Tucker	17	1824	Lace Maker	nr the Church
112	Edward	Upright	32	1809	Lace Maker	Church
113	Elizabeth	Ward	11	1830	Lace Maker	Berry Hill
114	Rachel	Whicker	15	1826	Lace Maker	Little Culverhole
115	Sarah	Woodgate	30	1811	Lace Maker	nr the Church
116	Caroline	Woodrow	24	1817	Lace Maker	Vicarage

APPENDIX 4

EXTRACT FROM THE COLYTON HUNDRED 1841 CENSUS

Taken from Online Historical population reports University of Essex http://www.histpop.org/ohpr/servlet/

Parish/ Tything	AREA	HOUSES			PERSONS			AGES				Persons Born	
	English Statute Acres	Inhabited	Un inhabited	Building	Males	Females	Total Persons	Under 20 Years		Over 20 Years		In this County	Else where
Branscombe	1750	178	4	0	452	504	956	231	248	221	256	911	45
Colyton	5430	479	36	1	1194	1257	2451	591	2590	603	667	2319	132
Cotleigh	1040	41	0	0	143	126	269	69	82	74	64	230	39
Farway	3420	59	1	0	205	171	376	102	74	103	97	355	21
Leigh, North	1450	48	1	0	137	115	252	74	57	63	58	234	18
Leigh, South	2130	67	1	0	189	168	357	101	78	88	90	349	8
Monkton	2090	26	0	0	75	66	141	35	33	40	33	137	4
Offwell	1200	82	2	1	229	209	438	114	97	115	112	396	42
Seaton	4120	146	16	1	337	428	765	166	196	171	232	648	117
Beer		254	5	1	536	695	1231	268	327	268	368	1171	60
Shute	1940	134	2	0	354	329	683	172	154	182	175	611	72
Widworthy	2840	45	0	0	137	120	257	58	51	79	69	240	17
	27410	1559	68	4	3988	4188	8176	1981	1967	2007	2221	7601	575

APPENDIX 5

Extract from the Will and Codicil of Jane Washbourne nee Bidney		
The approximate valuation of the net estate, in 2013, would have been approximately £280,000. Therefore £100 would be the equivalent of about £10,000 in 2013 and 4s would be the equivalent of £25		
LEGATEE	WILL	CODICIL
[1]Fanny Millard (niece of my said late Husband)	£100	
[2]Eliza Shard (niece of my said late Husband)	£300	
[3]Charles William Washbourne (the nephew of my said late Husband)	£200	
[4]to my cousin Hannah Clarke of Beer	£50	+£50
[5]my cousin Elizabeth Miller (Wife of Edwin Miller)	£50	+£50
[6]Annie Adams (formally Annie Hurdle) of Topsham	£30	
[7]Mary Lloyd Searle of Point in View Lympston (sic)	£20	
[8]Martha the wife of Benjamin William Webb	£100	
[9]Naney the Widow of the late John Symes who at the time of his death resided at 4 Peel Terrace Old Stafford near Manchester	£50	
[10]Elizabeth Maria, wife of John Frederick Knott of Staley Bank Staleybridge	£50	
[11,12]Martha Symes of Richmond Terrace Old Trafford Manchester	£100	Revoked
[13] Elizabeth the widow of my late friends the Reverend James Gwyther Three hundred pounds	£300	
[14]Congregational Church in Beer (to be invested in such securities and upon such trusts as my executor may consider most desirable for the promoting of the prosperity of that Church and the comfort of the Minister thereof for the time being)	£100	
[15]National Lifeboat Association to be used towards providing a Life Boat for Beer near Seaton	£100	

[16]James Gwyther my executor to be given by him as he may see fit to or amongst any person or persons who may be waiting on me in my last illness	£50	
[17]Ann Wife of Henry Miller, of Beer	4/s per month	Revoked
[12]Mary Driver, Spinster, of Beer	4/s per month	Revoked
[12]Caroline Lane, Spinster, of Beer	4/s per month	Revoked
[12] Elizabeth Searle, Spinster, of Beer	4/s per month	Revoked
[18]Agnes E Weston of Devonport the legacy of One hundred pounds to be used by her for the establishment of or maintenance of a Sailors Rest or Sailors Boys Home		£100

Footnotes:

1. Frances (Fanny) Millard was born in 1821; the daughter of Nathaniel's sister Frances and her husband Joseph.
2. Eliza Francis nee Washbourne was born in 1826; the daughter of Nathaniel's brother William and his wife Sophia. She married Charles Shard in 1851
3. Charles William Washbourne was born in 1845; the son of Nathaniel's brother Charles and his wife Matilda
4. Hannah was the daughter of William Clarke and Mary nee Bidney. Mary was Jane's paternal Aunt. Hannah was born circa 1839, in Awliscombe but in later life ran a Grocery, in Beer.
5. Jane's cousin Elizabeth Miller is shown with Jane on the 1841 Census at 76 Little St James Street, Westminster, London, as a Lace Manufacturer. It is therefore likely that Elizabeth was one of the women who helped to make Queen Victoria's wedding lace. Elizabeth Bidney Clarke was born in 1816 in Beer and married Edwin Miller in 1839 in St James Westminster. She was the daughter of William Clarke and Mary nee Bidney, (Mary was Jane's Aunt, her father's sister) and Elizabeth was sister of Hannah.
6. Ann Hurdle was born in 1822 in Topsham and married William Adams in 1866
7. Mary Lloyd Searle was baptised in 1806. On the 1841 Census, she was shown as a lace maker, living with Jane's stepmother Jane Bidney (Snr). It is possible that she too helped to make Queen Victoria's Wedding dress. In the 1861 census, she was shown as living at

"Point in View", Withycombe Raleigh.

8. Martha Turner was born about 1820 in Linkenholt, Hampshire and married Benjamin William Webb in 1841 in West Wickham.
9. Nancy nee Symes was Dr James Gwyther's maternal aunt.
10. Elizabeth Maria Knott nee Symes was Dr James Gwyther's maternal cousin.
11. Martha Symes, Dr James Gwyther's maternal aunt, had died between Jane making her initial will and her codicil. The amount originally left to her and her descendants was therefore revoked.
12. he amount originally left to these legatees and their descendants was revoked in Jane's codicil. It would seem that the money was instead left to "Aggie Weston's"; a legacy which was not part of Jane's original will.
13. Elizabeth Gwyver nee Symes. She died the year before Jane.
14. The Jane Washbourne Charity is still (2013) administered by the Beer Congregational Chapel: Charity No: 262661-
15. The RNLI confirm that they received Jane's Legacy and although no Lifeboat station was built in Beer and consequently Jane did not get her wish for a life boat for Beer.
16. Jane's executor was the son of her friends the Reverend James Gwyther and his wife Elizabeth.
17. Ann Miller, Mary Driver and Elizabeth Searle are shown as lace makers on the 1841 census in Beer. It is likely that they were some of the women who helped to make Queen Victoria's wedding lace.
18. Jane's Legacy of £100 helped to maintain "Aggie Weston's" Royal Sailors' Rests.

APPENDIX 6
Ida Allen Family Tree

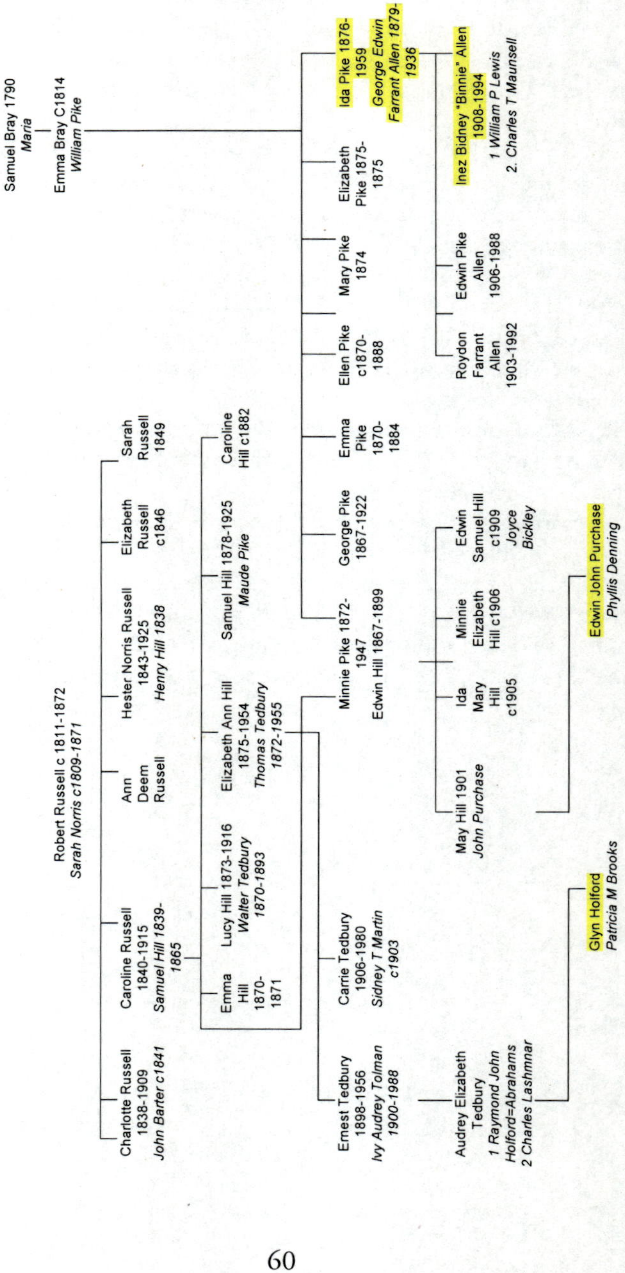

APPENDIX 7

Article Written by Ida Allen using the alias Primrose

172 *THE GIRL'S OWN PAPER.*

THE SECOND COMPETITION FOR GIRLS WHO WORK WITH THEIR HANDS.

FOURTH PRIZE ESSAY (£2 2s.).

MY DAILY ROUND.

DEAR MR. EDITOR

I have been thinking since I read your last Daily Round Competition letters that I should like to let you see a lace workers daily round, which work I have to earn my living by,

The summer is my busy time and I rise very early and get my little oil stove. ready and make a cup of tea and ready to sit down to work by 5 oclock sometimes earlier than that. I live quite alone in a little cottage facing the sea and cliffs, and as the days are so hot I like to have the early morning as I have to keep my work very clean so that it does not have to be washed before I sell it. I am to day doing point lace cuffs, and I work for the village shop people who give out the work ready tacked to the pattern they require, which first I draw around with needle and fine cotton in every pinhole of the braid; the pattern is covered with; then if we require a new pattern to work on again I place a sheet of paper over the work drawn and with a piece of heelbore, it is called, rub and the black marks comes on the clean paper, and then we have a new pattern, to begin another time, then I do a lot of buttonhole bars and pretty stitches which we have learnt, then the last stitch is called pearling; which is done with a coarser cotton, on the outside edge then we rip it off the paper; and take it to the shop, where I get things to make use of as we are not paid money there;

I sit to work untill 8 oclock then I get my breakfast and put my house tidy and if I have any dinner to cook I get all ready. I sit to work again by half past nine or ten sometimes then work untill 12 oclock, and if very busy for post as we call it, that is the work we are asked to do by a certain time; I do not stop only for a bread and cheese dinner and a cup of tea or an egg for we cannot afford meat dinners, every day I get fish and things very cheap in our village so it helps one a lot where we have not much money to spare, so after having my bit of dinner if not busy I take my book and sit down in the fields or indoors in my hour we have for dinner, Sometimes there are two of us have a piece of work between us so then I take my piece to a friends house to work alike or they come to mine and it is nice to have company at times so I get to work again and work until 4 oclock and then put on my little kettle on my oil stove which saves coal in Summer; and get my tea then sit to work until 8 o clock then I leave off and if I have not finished my peice; I then take my can to fetch my water and do any odd jobs I find to do; take my little can to a neighbours for her little girl to fetch my milk at the farm in the morning then I fetch other things I may want for my use and if I have time to go to see a dear old woman, who I call granny and who loves to talk to me, and then I go to see how much work my girl friend has done and then go home to my supper and book for living alone I love books they are my friends now I have lost my mother, Then I go to bed and before retiring I thank my Heavenly Father for his mercies which I enjoy which are many I am glad to say then if I am spared I begin my daily round each day but often get weary but glad to be able to get work to do The lace work is very trying to the sight and I am often very glad of an order from Ladies who pay money and a better price than what the shop people do for after working all day as I have said I earn but bare 7d and then only taken out in the shop

Ladies often send their Honiton Lace to be cleaned and put on new net; which is called transferring and then it will look like new lace; and that is real pillow lace which I have learnt; but it went down in price years agone and now if wanted they don't pay the full price for so the Point lace is done quicker and then we get really more for it We used in the village to have schools for teaching children the work but it does not do now they have to keep to the daily school and then they go to service, I have learnt all the different sorts and find it most useful now as I cannot live in service my knee gives out so glad to come home to the lace work.

A pair of cuffs takes two days and we get 1/2 for them or the worth of it in goods, so I hope if ever my daily round should be in print it will help to show the readers how hard some have to work to earn a shilling before they can spend it if we want clothes we have a book at the shop and they buy us what we want and we work on until we have paid for it.

All these statements I declare to be perfectly true—

"PRIMROSE."

Branscombe

Nr. Axminister

August 11th. Devon

APPENDIX 8

Names of Lace Makers/Workers from the Branscombe 1911 Census						
	First Name	Surname	Age	Born Circa	Occupation	Address
1	Lucy Edith	Abbott	24	1887	Lace Maker	Old Castle
2	Alice	Bartlett	25	1886	Lace Maker	Street
3	Samuel	Chick	69	1842	Dealer in hand made lace	Hazlewood
4	Elizabeth	Coombs	51	1860	Honiton Lace dealer	Collick House
5	Gertrude	Cox	24	1887	Point Lace Maker	Lower Dean
6	Olive	Cox	19	1892	Lace Maker Honiton	Lower Dean
7	Susan Ann	Cox	48	1863	Lace Maker Honiton	Lower Dean
8	Amelia	Dean	20	1891	Lace Maker	Culverhole
9	Rosina	Dean	43	1868	Honiton Lace Maker & Manufacturer	Sea View
10	Cora	Dowell	55	1856	Honiton Lace Maker	Blue Ball
11	Edith	Dowell	16	1895	Point Lace Maker	Blue Ball
12	Laura	Dowell	20	1891	Honiton Lace Maker	Blue Ball
13	Ann	Evans	46	1865	Lace Maker	Street
14	Agnes	Farrant	35	1876	Point Lace Maker	Street
15	Leavina	Farrant	43	1868	Lace Worker	Deems
16	Mildred	Farrant	49	1862	Honiton Lace Maker	Street
17	Sarah Jane	French	68	1843	Lace Maker	Bank
18	Abilgail	Gill	41	1870	Lace Maker	Bridge
19	Clara	Gill	52	1859	Lace Worker	Street
20	Mary Ann	Gill	75	1836	Lace Maker	Bank
21	Maud	Gill	37	1874	Honiton Lace Maker	Bridge
22	Susan	Gill	42	1869	Lace Maker	Bank
23	Susan	Gill	75	1836	Lace Maker	Bridge

24	Harriett	Gosling	35	1876	Honiton Lace Maker	Berry Hill Cottages
25	Caroline Louise	Gush	15	1896	Lace Maker	Vicarage
26	Emily	Gush	37	1874	Point Lace Maker	Seaside Road
27	Emma	Gush	81	1830	Lace Maker	Vicarage
28	Ida	Gush	25	1886	Lace Maker	Cliff View
29	Mary Jane	Gush	56	1855	Point Lace	Vicarage
30	Olive Sarah	Gush	17	1894	Honiton Lace Maker	Little Seaside
31	Alice E	Hansford	31	1880	Lace Maker	Bank
32	Emily	Hansford	28	1883	Lace Worker	Grapevine Cottages
33	Catherine	Harris	51	1860	Honiton Lace Maker	Street
34	Edith Mary	Hawker	31	1880	Lace Worker	Vicarage
35	Bertha Mary Ann	Lee	34	1877	Honiton Lace Maker	Baldash
36	Edith	Lee	85	1826	Honiton Lace Maker	Little Hooknell
37	Laura	Lee	21	1890	Honiton Lace Maker	Baldash
38	Lilllie	Lee	24	1887	Honiton Lace Maker	Baldash
39	Charlotte	Lockyer	36	1875	Lace Maker	Vicarage Hill
40	Elizabeth Ann	Lockyer	73	1838	Lace Maker	Vicarage Hill
41	Emma	Lockyer	53	1858	Lace Worker	Old Castle
42	Harriet	Loving	77	1834	Lace Worker	Street
43	Emmalene	Newton	56	1855	Honiton Lace Maker	Street
44	Alice	Northcott	21	1890	Lace Maker	Culverhole
45	Bessie	Northcott	41	1870	Lace Maker	Higher Church
46	Lydia	Northcott	77	1834	Honiton Lace Maker	Fern Cottage, Street
47	Daisy	Parratt	18	1893	Point Lace Worker	High Church

48	Elsie	Parratt	20	1891	Point Lace Worker	High Church
49	Nessa	Parratt	22	1889	Lace Maker	High Church
50	Elise	Perr	22	1889	Lace Maker	Vicarage
51	Dora	Perry	18	1893	Lace Maker	Vicarage
52	Kate	Perry	52	1859	Lace Maker	Vicarage
53	Kate Maria	Perry	18	1893	Lace Maker	Vicarage
54	Laura	Perry	16	1895	Lace Maker	Vicarage
55	Mary Jane	Perry	58	1853	Lace Maker	Vicarage
56	Bessie	Perryman	22	1889	Lace Maker	Cliff View Row
57	Jane	Perryman	33	1878	Lace Maker	Church Row
58	May Victoria	Perryman	15	1896	Lace Maker	Church Cottage
59	Nellie	Perryman	26	1885	Lace Maker	Cliff View Road
60	Sarah	Perryman	67	1844	Lace Maker	Church Row
61	Sidney	Perryman	20	1891	Lace Maker	Cliff View Road
62	Sophia	Perryman	14	1897	Lace Maker	Cliff View Road
63	Sarah Ann	Pike	25	1886	Lace Worker	Chapel Row
64	Elizabeth	Pile	71	1840	Lace Worker	Old Castle
65	Florence Emily	Quick	23	1888	Lace Maker	Little Seaside
66	Maryann	Raffill	68	1843	Lace Worker	Cott Cottages
67	Charlotte	Salter	67	1844	Lace Maker	Vicarage
68	Mary Ann	Salter	68	1843	Lace Maker	Vicarage

69	Beatrice	Sommers	16	1895	Honiton Lace Maker	Street
70	Maryann	Sommers	48	1863	Lace Worker	Street
71	Susanna	Somers	88	1823	Lace Maker	Bank Cottages
72	Maude	Snell	23	1888	Lace Maker	Cliff View
73	Elsie	Snell	21	1890	Lace Maker	Cliff View
74	Sarah	Ward	70	1841	Honiton Lace Maker	Blue Ball
75	Eliza	Williams	62	1849	Honiton Lace Maker	Church Road
76	Mary Ann	Woodrow	69	1842	Lace Maker	Grapevine Cottages
77	Tryphena	Wooddrow	29	1882	Point Lace Maker	Grapevine Cottages
78	Beatrice	Wyatt	33	1878	Lace Maker	Church Row

APPENDIX 9

Names of Lace Makers/Workers from the Beer 1911 Census						
	First Name	Surname	Age	Born Circa	Occupation	Address
			Honiton Lace			
1	Ellen	Abbott	59	1852	Point Lace Maker	2 Berry Lane
2	Sarah	Abbott	55	1856	Honiton Pillow Lace Maker	4 Rose Cottages
3	Maria	Agland	66	1845	Honiton Lace Maker	1 The Square
4	Sarah Jane	Agland	73	1838	Honiton Lace Maker	1 Berry Lane
5	Ida	Allen	34	1876	Honiton Lace Dealer	Branscombe House 8 Main Street
6	Elizabeth Ann	Bartlett	76	1835	Honiton Lace Maker	5 Sea View
7	Doris Ethel	Bryant	15	1896	Honiton Lace Maker (Learner)	2 Quarry Cottages
8	Mary Ann	Drew	62	1849	Lace Maker Honiton Pillow Lace	90 Main Street
9	Louisa	Driver	59	1852	Lace Maker Honiton Pillow Lace	1 Alms Houses
10	Mary Ann	Driver	62	1849	Lace Maker Honiton Pillow Lace	90 Main Street
11	Florence	Durrant	45	1866	Lace Maker Honiton Pillow Lace	1 York Place 46 Main Street
12	Martha	Gush	59	1852	Lace Maker Honiton	105 Main Street
13	Thomas William	Hammond	56	1855	Designer - Lace	Central Bakery 28 Main Street
14	Martha	Harrier	50	1861	Honiton Lace Maker	25 Main Street/ Fore Street
15	Mary Ann Harriet	Harvet	31	1880	Lace Maker Honiton	The Supply Stores 30 Main Street
16	Ida	Laptin	14	1897	Honiton Lace Worker	3 Hammetts Court 37 Main Street

17	Harriet	Hookings	69	1842	Lace Maker Honiton Pillow Lace	19 Main Street
18	Susan	Jenkinson	70	1841	Lace Maker Honiton Pillow Lace	4 Caddys Row
19	Augusta	Laptin	18	1893	Honiton Lace Worker	37 Main Street
20	Eliza	Marshall	75	1838	Honiton Lace Maker	4 Berry Lane
21	Sarah Ann	Miller	66	1845	Honiton Lace Maker	1 Lion Villa Cottages
22	Elizabeth	Newton	51	1860	Grocer & Honiton Lace Dealer	85 Main Street
23	Sarah Jane	Newton	50	1861	Dress Maker & Honiton Lace Instructor	2 Berry Lane
24	Jane	Perry	50	1861	Honiton Pillow Lace Worker	66 Main Street
25	Marie	Potter	69	1842	Lace Maker (Honiton)	Church Close 20 Main Street
26	Jane	Prescott	78	1833	Lace Dealer and Grocer	Diamond House 15 Main Street
27	Hannah	Restorick	54	1857	Honiton Lace Maker	40 Main Street
28	Violet Mary Letitia	Rodger	23	1888	Lace Maker Honiton Pillow Lace	2 Quarry Cottages
29	Maria	Russell	68	1843	Honiton Lace Maker	1 Hammetts Court
30	Alice M	Seaward	30	1881	Lace Maker Honiton Pillow Lace	19 Main Street
31	Sarah J	Seaward	72	1839	Lace Maker & Dealer	19 Main Street
32	Mary Ann	Thorn	61	1850	Honiton Lace Maker	64 Main Street
33	Emily Searle	Tizzard	76	1835	Honiton Lace Maker	8 Rose Cottage Clapps Lane
34	Elizabeth	Westlake	50	1861	Lace Maker Honiton	71 Main Street
35	Louisa Alice	Westlake	50	1861	Honiton Lace Maker	2 Windfield Terrace
36	Elizabeth Ann	White	69	1842	Honiton Lace Worker	Haselmere

37	Lydia	Woodgate	54	1857	Lace Maker Honiton	5 Alms Houses
38	Mary Ann	Woodgate	56	1855	Honiton Lace Worker	4 Clapps Lane
39	Mary Ann	Woodgate	70	1841	Honiton Lace Maker	5 Gordon Terrace
Honiton Lace – Retired						
1	Mary Ann	Bartlett	85	1826	Old Age Pensioner Former Honiton Lace Maker	4 Restoricks Court
2	Sarah	Board	76	1865	Old Age Pensioner Former Honiton Lace Maker	2 Alms Houses
3	Mary Ann	Lockyer	77	1834	Former Lace Worker	38 Main Street
4	Mary	Perry	85	1826	Formerly Lace Maker	3 Alms Houses
5	Tabitha	Thomas	82	1849	Formerly Honiton Lace Worker	1 Clapps Lane
6	Caroline	Westlake	80	1831	Old Age Pensioner Former Honiton Lace Maker	4 Restoricks Court
7	Anna Maria	Woodgate	73	1838	Old Age Pensioner Former Honiton Lace Maker	5 Berry Lane
8	Elizabeth Ann	Woodgate	85	1826	Old Age Pensioner Former Honiton Lace Maker	7 Caddys Row
Nottingham Lace						
1	Beatrice	Agland	17	1894	Plain Nottingham Net lace worker	6 Highfield House
2	Violet	Board	14	1897	Lace mender plain Nottingham net	2 Gospel Hall Court
3	Vina	Bond	28	1883	Plain Nottingham Net lace mender	5 Malt House Court
4	Gertrude	Driver	21	1890	Plain Nottingham Net lace mender	20 Clapps Lane

5	Phylis	Driver	18	1893	Net worker Plain Nottingham	93 Main Street
6	Rose	Pulman	19	1892	Plain Nottingham Net Lace mender	8 Highfield Terrace
7	Mabel	Pulman	13	1898	Plain Nottingham Net Lace mender	8 Highfield Terrace
8	Elizabeth Susan	Real	18	1893	Net mender Plain Nottingham	2 Caddys Row
9	Mary	Russell	21	1890	Lace mender Plain Nottingham	1 Hammetts Court
10	Mary	Westlake	26	1885	Brussels Net mender	41 Main Street
11	Mary Ann	Woodgate	31	1880	Plain Nottingham Net lace mender	5 Gordon Terrace
12	Elizabeth Ann	Woodgate	29	1882	Plain Nottingham Net lace mender	5 Gordon Terrace